T0195703

ON
EAGLES'
WINGS

FAITH, FORTITUDE, AND FAMILY

Bobbie J Hays

WESTBOW
PRESS®
A DIVISION OF THOMAS NELSON
& ZONDERVAN

WestBow Press books may be ordered through booksellers or by contacting:

WestBow Press
A Division of Thomas Nelson & Zondervan
1663 Liberty Drive
Bloomington, IN 47403
www.westbowpress.com
1 (866) 928-1240

Scripture taken from the King James Version of the Bible.

Scripture taken from the Amplified Bible, Copyright © 1954, 1958, 1962, 1964, 1965, 1987 by The Lockman Foundation. Used with permission.

Scripture taken from The Message. Copyright © 1993, 1994, 1995, 1996, 2000, 2001, 2002. Used by permission of NavPress Publishing Group.

ISBN: 978-1-9736-8941-6 (sc)
ISBN: 978-1-9736-8942-3 (e)

Library of Congress Control Number: 2020906960

Print information available on the last page.

WestBow Press rev. date: 04/22/2020

Ye have seen what I did unto the Egyptians, and how I bare you on eagles' wings, and brought you unto myself. Now therefore, if ye will obey my voice indeed, and keep my covenant, then ye shall be a peculiar treasure unto me above all people: for all the earth is mine: And ye shall be unto me a kingdom of priests, and an holy nation. These are the words which thou shalt speak unto the children of Israel. (Exodus 19:4–6 KJV)

You have seen what I did to the Egyptians, and how I carried you on eagles' wings, and brought you to myself. Now therefore, if you will in fact obey my covenant (agreement), then you shall be my one special possession and treasure from among all peoples (of the world), for all the earth is mine; and you shall be to Me a kingdom of priests and a holy nation (set apart for My purpose). These are the words that you shall speak to the Israelites. (Exodus 19:4–6 AMP)

CONTENTS

PREFACE

On Eagles' Wings, a book that deals with faith, fortitude, and family, was conceived many years ago while I was living with my sister- and brother-in-law and recuperating from a battle with depression and loss. While my sister (Ruby) and her husband (Derrick) were at work, I took advantage of the time by using their computer. It was a very dark period in my life, yet God allowed me to make use of this time. It also was a way to reassure my family that I wasn't idle during the day.

As the Holy Spirit gave me the book, along with my revisions, I give it to you now. I pray that these nuggets of truth will bless your life as they have blessed mine.

Concerning *faith*, *Roget's Thesaurus* says that it is the absolute certainty in the trustworthiness of another. Many have already put their trust in our Lord and Savior, Jesus Christ. We call that having faith in the trustworthiness of Christ. What he did at Calvary was sufficient to save our souls. The fact that he died, was buried, and rose from the grave assures us that one day, we too will rise and spend eternity with God.

On a daily basis, we exercise our faith from the time we get up in the morning until we go to sleep at night. With each decision we make and each prayer we pray, we are exercising faith. The important thing to remember when trusting is who the object of our faith is.

Fortitude means that the quality of mind enabling one to face danger or hardship resolutely (not hesitating or wavering). Once we have accepted Christ as our Savior, we have taken on an unwavering course of action. We have made a decision to accept and demonstrate our power to make choices, to set goals, and to act upon them firmly, despite opposition or difficulty. We have the Lord's promise that he will never leave or forsake us (See Hebrews 13:5 KJV). We have the promise that he that has begun a good work in us will perform it until the day of Jesus Christ (See Philippians 1:6 KJV).

God has blessed us with the gift of *family*. Some believe that a family is a group of people who shares a common ancestry. Usually, it is a group of related people who are living together as a unit. It pertains to those living within the household. Family is a foundational institution of society that has been ordained by God. It is constituted by marriage and is composed of persons who are related to one another through marriage, blood, or adoption. The family is a fundamental institution of human society (See Genesis 2:20–25; 4:1; Exodus 20:5–6; Joshua 7:10, 15, 24–25; 2 Kings 13:23 KJV).

ACKNOWLEDGMENTS

I thank and honor our Lord and Savior, Jesus Christ, who by his Holy Spirit, inspired me to put these thoughts into print. Many people have touched my life in positive ways. I acknowledge and appreciate them for sharing their love with me. I especially thank my siblings for believing in me and giving me space.

To my living siblings, Leroy, Ruby, Chauncey, Randy, Milton, Joyce, Jackie, and Marvin, may each of your lives be daily enriched and blessed with God's mercy and grace. Be certain that you have accepted Jesus Christ as your Lord and Savior and that you are walking in the light of his love. Always take time to give something back and to bless others. That's the price that we pay for living on this great planet. Thank you for your kindness toward me and for sharing your successes, joys, sorrows, and failures. I love you and your families.

To our third oldest sibling, Bruce, who was a source of joy to the older generation, which was evident at the time of your going home, I am certain that we all still miss you. God saw fit to take you home at an early age, despite the fact that you had two precious children whose eyes lit up whenever they saw you. Although we sometimes felt threatened by your rough play, we still loved and respected you. We were torn up by your untimely and tragic death.

To our dear deceased mother, Muddear, there is no love like a mother's love. Thank you for having enough love to spread over all of us. You taught us to be thankful for what we consider the *little things* in life.

I married the man of my dreams. We were blessed with two amazing sons, Thado Nakia and Terrance Nathan, both of whom have added joy and purpose to my life. I love you guys, your spouses, Terika and Turkeesha, and each of my grandchildren, who occupy a special place in my heart. To my extended family, your love has proven genuine all these years. Thank you, Terika, for assisting me with technology.

I acknowledge my spiritual leaders and my spiritual families, from the past and the present, which have encouraged, prayed for, and supported me in so many ways. I am a better person for having been graced with your friendships. To my Mississippi friends—you know whom you are—you are the best. To my godmother, Barbara Wheatley, your love has inspired and encouraged me down through the years. Thank you.

To God be the glory!

PROCRASTINATION

I can do all things through Christ which strengthens me.

—Philippians 4:13 (KJV)

I knew that each day that I failed to pick up my pen was costing me my freedom. I believed that God would produce a hundredfold harvest in my life, yet I was trapped inside myself. Does this sound familiar?

Procrastination can be costly. We keep putting something off until it costs us more in the long run. We put off our physical exams, only later to find that we now need surgeries, which could have been avoided if we had only attended to our health issues sooner.

Another way procrastination can cost us is through when we put off assignments until the last minute. The assignment would have had a more flavorful and vibrant touch had it been done days or weeks earlier. The saying, "Don't put off until tomorrow what you can do today," certainly has its place in the lives of procrastinators.

2

STEP OUT AND ONTO FAITH

Faith is believing that God is in the dark as well as in the light. He is the same in both.

Faith is the substance of things hoped for and the evidence of things that have not yet been seen. When a child of God steps out and onto faith, he or she is saying to the world, "I know that God is able to hold me up no matter how things look on the outside. Within me, I am holding on because outside of me, I'm being held up by faith in an all-wise and all-knowing God.

Each day, we take a faith walk. When we walk by faith and not by sight, we can step out of our boats of security and have blessed assurance that we will not go under. God is able to keep us from falling, no matter how strong or fierce the tide is.

One day, Peter stepped out of the boat and onto faith and attempted to meet Jesus at his point of reckoning. However, I believe that because Peter took his eyes off Jesus and looked at his surroundings, at that moment, his faith became shallow. When the Lord extends his hand to us and bids us to come (See Matthew 14:29 KJV), we must keep our focus on him.

Faith helps us to come to grips with things that may not be working in our favor. Faith bids us to try new things we are passionate about. When we are not making progress, faith tells us to loosen our grip and to try something else. When something doesn't work, we don't need to hold on to it and to become dormant. We must let go and let God. Today, I challenge you to step out on faith.

3

MOUNT UP

> But they that wait upon the Lord shall renew their strength; they shall mount up with wings as eagles; they shall run, and not be weary; they shall walk and not faint.
>
> (Isaiah 40:31 KJV)

A flock of gray birds was trying to get into flight formation. Many of the birds appeared to be disturbed because the lead bird was flying too low and the flock could not move forward. Each time, they kept forming, lifting up, and ending up right back where they had started.

When standards or goals for an establishment or an organization are too low, its workers or groups cannot move forward to accomplish assigned tasks. The birds that were trying to form kept falling to the ground in frustration. They were flapping their wings and running into each other. This happens in groups when team members cannot exercise their faith, God-given talents, and gifts and walk with God.

The leader who becomes tired or burned out does not have to quit. It is usually in the best interests of the group if the leader falls back and lets someone else take the lead. Notice that I said falls *back* and not falls *out*. That is what the flock of gray birds did when they finally got off the ground. When the lead bird became worn out, it fell back, and the next bird in line took the lead.

Now, only the bird that has been following the leader closely is able to lead next. You see, in order to be a good leader, one must first be a good follower. Jesus said to his disciples, "Follow me" (Matthew 9:9 KJV).

It was truly amazing to watch those large gray birds. I wanted desperately to help them out, but I did not speak their language … or did I? I spent half the night thinking about it. I prayed that no plane would fly low enough to hinder those huge gray birds from flying south.

4

CARE FOR THE POOR

Blessed is he that considereth the poor; for the Lord will deliver him in times of trouble.

—Psalm 41:1 (KJV)

The Bible says that caring for the poor is lending to the Lord and that we will be repaid well (See Proverbs 19:17 KJV). When Christians take time out of their busy schedules to care for God's people, God is happy with that. He especially wants us to care for the poor. It is just like loaning God something. We are always to care for the poor and those who are downtrodden and distressed.

The Word of God says, "Whoso stoppeth his ears at the cry of the poor, he also shall cry himself, but shall not be heard" (Proverbs 21:13 KJV). The Word also says, "But whoso hath this world's good, and seeth his brother have need, and shutteth up his bowels of compassion from him, how dwelleth the love of God in him?" (1 John 3:17 KJV).

The Lord wants us not only to pray for others but also to be the answer to some of those prayers. Many times, people think the Lord doesn't answer their prayers. Sometimes it's because some of us are not obedient when the Holy Spirit tells us to be the answer.

The Message Bible phrases it this way, "If you see some brother or sister in need and have the means to do something about it but turn a cold shoulder and do nothing, what happens to God's love? It disappears. And you make it disappear" (1 John 3:17).

In Luke 4:18, Jesus says, "The Spirit of the Lord is upon me because he has chosen me to tell the good news to the poor. The Lord has sent me to proclaim liberty for prisoners, to give sight to the blind, to free everyone who suffers, and to say, This is the year the Lord has chosen" (KJV).

We are to take God at his word by doing what he left us to do. When we do, we are rewarded for our obedience and our effort. He may not always reward us monetarily. The Lord rewards his people in numerous ways. He gives us peace, joy, happiness, courage, material blessings, healing from diseases, and forgiveness of sins. He protects us from death, provides for our needs, and gives us the strength of a young eagle. The Lord always brings justice for all who are mistreated.

Our God can be trusted. While we care for the poor, the Lord takes care of our affairs and moves in our lives in ways that we could never imagine. I challenge you today. If the Spirit has asked you to give of your time or resources to help some soul, do it. You will be amazed at God's goodness toward you.

5

TRUST GOD

Trust in the Lord with all thine heart; lean not unto thine own understanding. In all thy ways acknowledge him; and he shall direct thy path.

—Proverbs 3:5–6 (KJV)

God is our Father. He is aware of everything that is going on in our lives. David says in Psalm 139, "Thou knowest my downsitting and mine uprising; thou understands my thoughts afar off. There is nowhere we can go where God is not" (Psalm 139:2 KJV).

I awoke one Valentine's Day morning and asked the Lord to surprise me. I got dressed at around noon and went to a restaurant for lunch. When I asked the waitress for my check, she told me it had already been taken care of by someone who had just left.

That morning, God saw deep inside my heart. He knew what I was really concerned about: how my day would be celebrated because I was not married or dating. However, what I failed to realize was that I was the bride of Christ.

Once on New Year's Eve before I left home to attend a worship service, I explained to the Holy Spirit that at midnight, parishioners would be embracing, and other ministers would be hugging their spouses. I asked him what I would be doing. He didn't answer me right away, but when I arrived at the service, the pastor asked if I would take charge, encourage the saints, and give the closing prayer. At midnight, I was praising the Father and talking to him on behalf of the congregation, when I had been concerned about what I would be doing.

Baby steps of faith are important to God. We walk by faith and not by sight, "for without faith it is impossible to please him" (Hebrews 11:6 KJV).

Other times, I've tried to help God out. He tells me to trust him. I say to you, trust God. Do not, by any means, lean on your own understanding. Our heavenly Father knows what we need even before we ask.

6

DISCIPLINE

Now no chastening for the present seemeth to be joyous, but grievous; nevertheless afterwards it yieldeth the peaceable fruit of righteousness unto them which are exercised thereby.

—Hebrews 12:11 (KJV)

The noun *discipline* according to Roget's Thesaurus means control gained by enforcing obedience or order; orderly or prescribed conduct or pattern of behavior; self-control. The verb *discipline* means to train; bring to a condition of order and obedience; bring under control.

"The Lord disciplines him whom he loves, and chastises every son whom he receives ... if you are left without discipline then you are illegitimate children and not sons" (Hebrews 12:6–8 KJV). When we fall under the Lord's judgment, he is disciplining us to save us from being condemned with the rest of the world (See 1 Corinthians 11:32 KJV).

The motive for discipline is love. Its purpose is salvation. The people of Israel muttered treason against the Lord and said, "It is because the Lord hated us that he brought us out of Egypt" (Deuteronomy 1:27 KJV). Although they had been freed from slavery, they were missing their onions. (See Numbers 11:5). Even though, they were led by the Lord of Hosts himself, his angels, and pillars of cloud and fire, they were terrified of the Amorites.

Discipline or chastening can be a painful thing for us poor mortals. We think only of the rod itself—the hard experience, the prayer that was answered with a no, the shattered hope, the misunderstanding, and the blow to our pride. We forget the loving hand that administers the lesson, our Savior, who leads us like a shepherd. We forget how much we need his tender care.

7

FROM THE WORD OF GOD

God hath spoken once; twice have I heard this; that power belongeth unto God.

—Psalm 62:11 (KJV)

Thy Word is a lamp unto my feet, and a light unto my path.

—Psalm 119:105 (KJV)

For God speaketh once, yea twice, yet man perceiveth it not. In a dream, in a vision of the night, when deep sleep falleth upon men, in slumberings upon the bed; Then he openeth the ears of men, and sealeth their instructions. That he may withdraw man from his purpose and hide pride from man. He keepeth back his soul from the pit, and his life from perishing by the sword.

—Job 33:14–18 (KJV)

God speaks to people when their senses are locked in sleep. He opens the ears of humans. He reveals or uncovers important information. He communicates valuable truths.

Sometimes, you intend to do something wrong, and in a dream, God will warn you that this will not be favorable for you. Dire consequences come with this. Take his path instead.

Tell me something. Has God spoken to you lately? He delights in speaking to his children. He often speaks to us in dreams and visions. He removes the wax of the world from our ears so that we may hear him.

I challenge you to read his Word. When you do, he will speak. When you commune with him in prayer, he will answer. When you share your faith, he will reward you.

8

SELAH

Be still and know that I am God.

—Psalm 46:10 (KJV)

Be still. Be quiet. Hush. Stop all the rushing around. Be still and know that he is God. The creator of the universe wants a word with you, but how can he talk to you if you are always on the go? Chill out and listen.

It takes a lot of focused effort to quiet the mind. The mind is always busy with one thought after another. They crowd the soul with decisions and things that need to be done. Why don't you shut all of it off and hear what your soul speaks to you?

Sometimes we have to shut it off, even though it may be a good message. Our minds need rest. They need time to refresh, reinvigorate, and rejuvenate. So whatever it is, lay it aside and listen for a while. Prepare your heart to receive from God and to hear his voice on a regular basis. Finally, acknowledge him in everything you do. Make being identified with Jesus Christ a lifestyle. Be a faithful doer of the Word.

Bobbie J Hays

Share

Encourage

Love

Acknowledge

Hush

9

Don't Stop Praying

Pray without ceasing.

—1 Thessalonians 5:17 (KJV)

When we pray without ceasing, we are always conscious of prayer. Sometimes we can get distracted by our to-do lists, the cares of this life, and the deceitfulness of riches. Later, we find that for hours, we have not even thought about God.

Prayer will do some powerful things. Prayer helps the church breathe properly. Some things happen in a church setting that stifle the very breath of the church. One of these things is the lack of prayer. Prayer is the very breath that keeps things moving forward. Just as we breathe in and out over and over again, we talk to God over and over again. Prayer revitalizes ministries in the church. It helps to keep them from folding and going under. Nothing moves ministry forward like studying and applying the Word and prayer.

I recall being at a revival where a group of saints in an upper room was praying for the evangelist the entire time the service was taking place. This went on each night of the revival. The praying saints did not reveal themselves until after the revival had ended. I'm not insinuating that others were not praying, but sometimes we are even more successful when we focus on a specific task without distractions.

The Bible tells us in Acts 4:31, "And when they had prayed the place was shaken where they were assembled together; and they were all filled with the Holy Ghost, and they spake the word of God with boldness" (KJV).

Prayer helps the church stay alert. It helps the church be on guard against deception. Prayer helps us to stay focused. Many things can pull us off our task. When we try to stay in touch with everything that is going on around us, we can easily lose our focus.

In Matthew 26:41, Jesus tells us to watch and pray. We must stay alert because the thief comes to kill, steal, and destroy us. Jesus has come so that we can have abundant life (See John 10:10 KJV). By watching and praying, we realize when the enemy is about to creep in.

Prayer aids the church in fulfilling its specific task. The early church continued steadfastly to study the apostles' doctrine and to fellowship with one another. They ate and prayed together. They feared God, and many wonders and signs were done by the apostles (See Acts 2:42–43 KJV).

We cannot expect to fulfill any task successfully without talking to God about it first. We should thank him while we are doing it and for his help when it's done. Don't stop praying.

10

WITHOUT CONTROVERSY

Forgetting those things which are behind…

— Philippians 3:13c (KJV)

The inception of "Without Controversy" came to mind during a reading of 1 Timothy. In this small book, the writer wishes to refresh our memory. He wants to awaken our spirits to the many great stories and events that have been and are continuing to be told and listened to, as though it had only happened yesterday.

> But if I tarry long, that thou mayest know how thou oughtest to behave thyself in the house of God, which is the church of the living God, the pillar and ground of the truth. And without controversy great is the mystery of godliness; God was manifested in the flesh, justified in the Spirit, seen of angels, preached unto the Gentiles, believed on in the world, received up into glory. (1 Timothy 3:15–16 KJV)

The great mystery is how God did what he did. He took a woman who had never had sexual relations, impregnated her by the power of the Holy Spirit, and desired her to walk around without shame on her part (Her husband-to-be had some problems until God sent an angel to him). God allowed Mary to be visited by an angel, to go through a full term of pregnancy, and later to give birth in a place that was not even fit for the goats, pigs, and other animals (See Luke 1:28; 2:7 KJV).

When others saw, by way of stars and so forth, what was happening these things were unexplainable because they were mysteries. How could anyone explain them except for the one who made them happen?

The virgin birth was and still is a mystery. No matter how much schooling one has or how many degrees one holds, it is still a mystery. One has to get power from a holy God to be able to tell the story of the virgin birth, the crucifixion, and the resurrection, not to mention the ascension on high. The resurrection would take forever to tell if it were ever told with all the authority that God offers.

11

A MYSTERY

Keep your eyes on the prize.

Behold, I show you a mystery (a secret) we shall not all sleep, but we shall all be changed. How shall it happen? In a moment in the twinkling of an eye, at the last trump; for the trumpet shall sound, and the dead shall be raised incorruptible and we shall be changed. For this corruptible must put on incorruption, and this mortal must put on immortality. These things have to be that the saying might be brought to pass, "Death is swallowed up in victory. O Death, where is thy sting? O Grave, where is thy victory? But thanks be to God, which giveth us the victory through our Lord Jesus Christ.

—1 Corinthians 15:51–57 (KJV)

Therefore, my beloved brethren, be ye steadfast, unmoveable, always abounding in the work of the Lord, forasmuch as ye know that your labour is not in vain in the Lord.

—1 Corinthians 15:58 (KJV)

The apostle Paul was letting the church know that flesh and blood cannot inherit the kingdom of God, so we should not get wrapped up in it. Just as we bear the image of the earth (the dirt), we are also going to bear the image of heaven. Right now, we're in transition. I agree with the songwriter who says that time on this earth is filled with swift transition, nothing on earth unmoved can stand; we should build our hopes on things eternal, and hold to God's unchanging hand.

God wants to tell and show you a secret. What is it? *We* will not all sleep, but we will be changed (See 1 Corinthians 15:51 KJV). Not all of us will die. Whether we're dead or alive when the Lord comes, we will be changed. We who are alive and remain until the coming of the Lord will not go before those who are asleep (See 1 Thessalonians 4:15 KJV). God has planned it all out. We should not be surprised when these things happen.

When our mom passed away, it came as no surprise—I knew it was going to happen but did not know how. Let me rephrase that. I did not know how it would happen. Oh, but our God knew. Since the day we were born, he has known how we will leave this world. That's why he doesn't want us to become too attached to it.

Now that we have been washed by his blood, we are no longer from here. This world is not our home. We're just passing through on our way to a better place—a place where the wicked will one day cease from troubling us, the weary will be at rest, and all of us who believe in Jesus are going to sit at his feet and to be blessed.

When will this happen? It will happen in a moment, in the twinkling of an eye, and when the last trumpet sounds (See 1 Corinthians 15:52 KJV). How can this happen? This piece of earth that is corruptible must become incorruptible. This mortal must put on immortality (See 1 Corinthians 15:53 KJV). It is a mystery.

12

LORD, GIVE ME PATIENCE, RIGHT NOW!

Do you want patience? If so, get ready for some tribulations. Patience, my friend, is a virtue, which only God, through the power of the Holy Spirit, can develop in us. We can kick and scream for days, and patience will not come because it has to be developed in the believer. This can take a while. Don't try to rush it. Just *be patient*.

When our faith is tested, patience is at work in us. James 1:1–3 says,

> My brethren, count it all joy when ye fall into divers temptations; knowing this, that the trying of your faith worketh patience. But let patience have her perfect work, that ye may be perfect and entire, wanting nothing. (KJV)

Whenever a believer asks God for patience, that person can expect his or her faith to be tested. It is not up to us to determine how long this process will take. It may take hours, weeks, months, or even years for patience to be perfected in a life.

One of the most important things a child of God can do when being tested is to focus on the end result rather than on what things look like at that moment. In Ecclesiastes 7:8, we find these words, "Better is the end of a thing than the beginning thereof: and the patient in spirit is better than the proud in spirit" (KJV). It is the end result that is going to matter in the long run.

Jesus is the author and the finisher of our faith, who for the joy that was set before him endured the cross, despising the shame. He is now sitting at the right hand of the throne of God. What would have happened if he had given up when things got rough? (and they did get rough). He focused on the joy that would ultimately be the outcome of his suffering, not for his own good but for ours. He wanted the joy of seeing us make it to where he was. He showed us that it could be done.

The first time I was led to teach a lesson on patience, it was a frightening experience for me. I was scheduled to teach a Bible class the next day, and the Holy Spirit hadn't given me a topic yet. I read and studied some scriptures on patience, which I thought were for me personally.

The next morning, I awoke and said, "Well, Lord, what am I going to talk about today?" There was no answer. I waited and waited until it was time for me to go. I thought to myself, *Maybe we'll just pray, and then I'll dismiss them.* Then it came to me, *Teach a lesson on patience.* There was no way I could have taught a lesson on patience if it had not manifested itself in me first. The next week, the same thing happened. I waited and waited. I realized that I was supposed to finish my series on patience. Sometimes we just have to wait.

The psalmist David phrased his words on patience so beautifully when he said, "I waited patiently for the Lord; and he inclined unto me and heard my cry" (Psalm 40:1 KJV). It was because David waited that the Lord heard his cry. How did he wait? He waited patiently. He did not wait in a fretful state, but instead, he waited patiently. It is one thing to wait and another thing to wait patiently. Lord, give me patience, right now!

13

Be Encouraged

The way up is down.

He sent a man before them, even Joseph, who was sold for a servant; whose feet were fettered in iron. The word of the Lord tried him. The king sent and loosed him, even the ruler of the people and let him go free; He made him (Joseph) lord of his house and ruler of all his substance: to bind his princes at his pleasure and teach his senators wisdom.

—Psalm 105:17,22 (KJV)

In his sermon "The Master Dreamer," L. Venchael Booth (*Outstanding Black Sermons*, Editor J. Alfred Smith Sr.) says,

Jealousy blinds the eyes, darkens the soul, and kills the spirit of love. It is a tragic waste of time to envy another because of his talents, his treasure, or his good fortune. God is the giver of these things, and you have no control over them. These brothers had within their hearts the seeds of destruction and were destined to live with the heaviness of their guilt. They give us a classic example that whatever is done to hurt, hurts the "hurter" more than the one who is hurt.

Joseph suffered many things before becoming lord of the palace. It was necessary that he be thrown into a pit so that he could rise to lead the palace.

Sometimes we have to go down before we can be elevated. Our Lord and Savior was battered, bruised, killed, and buried in a borrowed tomb so that he could be raised to sit at the right hand of the Father and to intercede for you and for me.

When we must go down, it gives us a testimony of how the Lord can and will deliver and set us free. When the Lord frees us, we are free indeed.

We see how the Hebrew boys, who refused to bow down to king Nebuchadnezzar, were thrown into a fiery furnace. Then the Lord showed up to rescue them, and not a hair on their heads was singed. The Lord will deliver us right on time. He may not always come when we expect him to come, but he is always on time. Be encouraged. God knows. He sees. He cares.

MEMORIES OF CHILDHOOD
DAYS AT MAMA'S HOUSE

I have many fond memories of my childhood days at Mama's house. At Mama's house, things were always so warm, neat, and cozy. For some reason, even the food tasted better at Mama's house. It wasn't that the food was truly better but because we were at Mama's house.

At Mama's house, we got to sit on her bed. We had to climb up because the bed was so high and the mattress was so firm.

Whenever we were alone with Mama and away from our other siblings, we'd ask, "Mama, can I spend the night with you?"

Her reply was always, "Yes, but you better ask your mother."

That child was some kind of special when he or she got the chance to spend the night at Mama's house. To spend the night with Mama meant that you had to sleep in her bed with her. Because Mama was a little heavy, when you climbed up on her bed, you'd just roll right under her. You talkin' bout warm!

Mama would always have something good like a cookie or a whining ball stashed away. We even got to turn the knobs on Mama's radio.

At Mama's house, we got the chance to go through her whatnots and look at miniature Coke bottles and crystal cats.

One day we found an x-ray of Uncle Howard's broken jawbone. We would try on Mama's jewelry, her usher's gloves, and her felt hats. Before long, we would hear Mama say, "Now put that right back like you found it."

Once, we thought that we were doing Mama a big favor and threw away many of the things she cherished. Mama didn't whip often, but boy when she did, my how it hurt!

At Mama's house, we had to say our prayers, and sometimes Mama would say, "That was too quick! Get right back down there and say 'em right!"

Mama has gone to be with the Lord. She fought a good fight. She kept the faith. She finished her course. Here is a piece that was penned in loving memory of our grandmother, Laura Griffin (Mama).

15

HE SIGNED MY NAME

MY TESTIMONY OF FAITH IN CHRIST

For Thou are my hope, O Lord God: Thou art my
trust from my youth.

—Psalm 71:5 (KJV)

When I was a young girl, I would often sneak under our house
to read the Bible. I especially enjoyed reading from the book of
Deuteronomy. Why, I do not recall.

One night during Easter week, I watched a movie about the
resurrection of Christ. I saw Jesus hanging on a cross bleeding,
and my heart ached for him. I saw in that movie where Jesus was
buried in a borrowed tomb. On the third day, he actually rose
from the dead. I recall being really upset because some of the
other characters in the movie did not believe that Jesus had risen.

When I was nine years old, I was told that if one wanted to
become a Christian, one would need to get on the mourners'
bench. During a revival at our church, if a person got off this
bench too soon, the elders would say that he did not have true
religion. If a person got off on the last night of a revival, they

would say that he only got off the bench because it was the last night.

So after talking it over with my oldest brother, who was also on the mourners' bench, I decided that I was going to get off on Thursday night. He agreed that we would do so too.

Well, we had a cousin who kept making attempts each night to get up from the bench. My brother and I laughed surreptitiously of course, because we believed that our cousin wanted attention.

Whenever a kid moved from the bench to the chair, that child was asked, "Have you got anything?" or "Do you have anything?" Well, I didn't know if I had a thing. I just believed that Jesus died for my sins and that he was buried and rose up from the grave.

Now, at that point in my life, I was not really associating all of this with God's unconditional love for me. I merely knew that at Easter, we sang the hymn "He Arose" and that it was true. I thought that everybody should believe that. After all, did they not see how he got up in the movie?

All of us finally got off the mourners' bench. When service ended, we were embraced. We were the talk of the neighborhood for the next few days. We were told that on the following Sunday, we would be baptized.

Sunday came, and we were decked out in pure-white gowns, a new white handkerchief on our heads, and a pure-white sheet, which we would be wrapped in when we came up out of the water. We lined up as our families and other church members watched from the top of the hill. We marched down the hill singing, "Take me to the water to be baptized."

The pastor and a couple of deacons reached for us one by one. This was a really wonderful experience; however, I did not feel that *thing* that others say I should have felt.

Time progressed, and we moved to another community where I met my friend, Shirley B. Now Shirley B. got on the mourners' bench during a revival one summer. Because she was my friend, I wanted to be baptized with her, but I was reminded that I had already been baptized.

Time progressed, and one thing led to another: junior high school, high school, college, marriage, children, jobs, and divorce. Soon I began to wrestle with the idea of whether or not I was saved. I watched a friend of mine walk in such peace. As a result, I started to question her about it.

She told me, "You have to let the Lord lead and guide you. Let him take control of your life."

I said to her, "Be a Christian, you mean?"

Well, I was a Christian, but I did not want to be one who had to do everything right, not even for a day. I could not do it. I would not do it. There was no way I could stop enjoying myself. I knew that I was already a Christian. I was just outside of church fellowship. I had no church family, no one to care about me and pray with me, and no one with whom I could study the Bible.

Upon entering church one Sunday, I took my usual seat on the back pew just in time to hear the hymn "Amazing Grace." I loved this song. I decided to walk down the aisle that Sunday and let the pastor know that I wanted to unite with the church. I had already been baptized, and I knew and loved Jesus.

Later, I struggled with a calling to preach the gospel. After months of swimming in the Word, soaking up everything that I possibly could from it, praying morning, noon, and night, and asking the Lord over and over if He actually wanted me to tell people about Him and what He had done and could do for them, I finally accepted the call.

Time progressed, and I began to become uncertain about my salvation. I wanted to know without a shadow of a doubt whether I was saved. So I asked, *Lord, am I saved? Everybody else has a story.*

They know when, where, and all of that. I want to know so that I can have a story to tell as well.

Wouldn't you know that the words, "Ask and it shall be given," became real to me? While I was sitting at my desk one day reading a little Gideon Bible, the Holy Spirit himself literally and voluntarily took hold of my hand and put it in my purse. It came out with a pen. I wrote my name in the back of that little Gideon Bible and dated it July 5, 1994, in the most *beautiful* penmanship I had ever seen.

He then led me to Ephesians 2:8, which reads, "For by grace are ye saved through faith; and that not of yourselves: it is the gift of God" (KJV). I then felt that my name had been written in the Lamb's Book of Life.

I came home that afternoon and fell down on my knees. The Holy Spirit began to love on me and minister to me like I had never before experienced it. I knew then that the Lord Jesus truly, truly loved me, and I received and accepted his love. I have been saved, sanctified, and filled with the precious Holy Spirit. *He signed my name.*

My Prayer for You

Dear heavenly Father, thank you for saving all who put their trust in you as their Lord and Savior. I am grateful that you have saved me and that you are preparing a home for me so that I may one day spend eternity with you. Please bless all who read this book and touch their lives so that they will come to know you in a very special and intimate way. Lord, I pray that our lives will be enriched daily, as we seek to know you in a more intimate way. I submit this prayer in the name of Jesus. Amen.

A Prayer of Salvation

Do you know beyond a shadow of a doubt that you are saved? If not, won't you pray this prayer?

> Lord, I am a sinner in need of your grace. Forgive my sins. I ask you to come into my life and to live in my heart. I accept you by faith as my Lord and Savior. I ask you to fill me with your precious Holy Spirit.
>
> I believe that you died for my sins and for the sins of the entire world. I believe that you died, that you were buried, and that on the third day, you rose from the dead. Thank you for saving me. In Jesus's name, I pray. Amen.

ABOUT THE AUTHOR

Bobbie J Hays is a native of Clarksdale, Mississippi. She is a retired teacher, minister, and workshop leader. She has two grown sons, Thado Nakia and Terrance Nathan. She has eight terrific, intelligent, and energetic grandchildren: Aviance, Makayla, Kierstain, Thado Jeremiah, Mason, Kayden, Terrance Jr., and Major.

She resided for twenty-seven years on the Mississippi Gulf Coast in Biloxi, Mississippi, where she got her start in the ministry and the teaching profession. After retirement, she moved to Florida to be near her sons, daughters-in-law, and grandchildren.

As a child, Bobbie recalls loving this man named Jesus. She later accepted Christ as Lord and Savior after the tragic death of her brother and the suicide of her mother.

Bobbie has a heart of compassion for the bereaved, brokenhearted, and the oppressed. She is a master grief mentor, who has been certified by Grief Care Fellowship Inc. She has served in that capacity at her local church.

Bobbie graduated from Coahoma Agricultural High and Coahoma Junior College. She is a 1972 graduate of Jackson State College. She attended two years of graduate school at the University of Mobile's School of Religion.

Bobbie has served as a minister to single adults and as a chairperson and organizer for Grief and Divorce Recovery Ministry. She is grateful to God for allowing her the opportunity to write and publish *On Eagles' Wings,* which has been a dream of hers for quite some time.

May all who read this book be as blessed reading it as she was writing it. To God be the glory!

Printed in the United States
By Bookmasters